I0831066

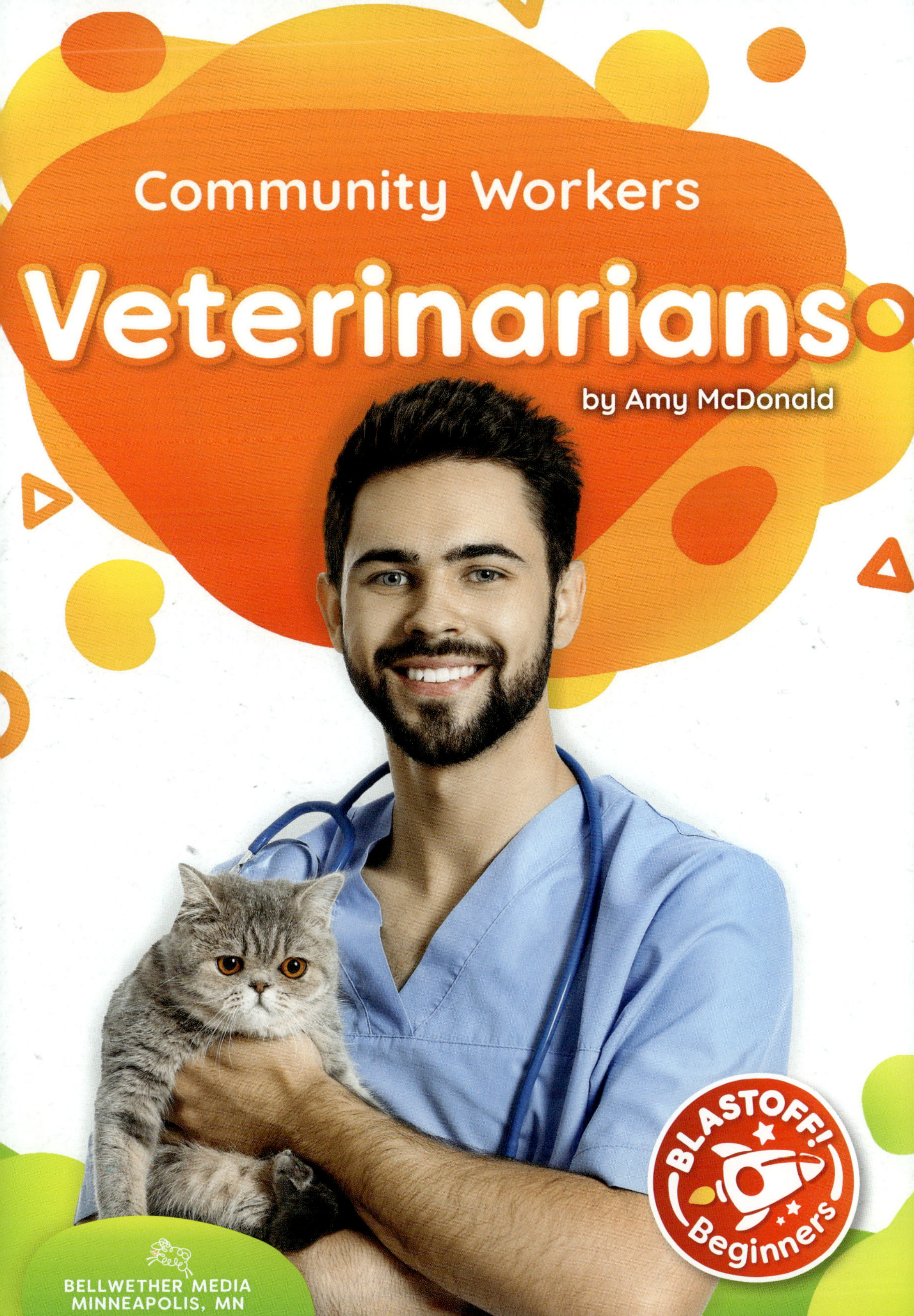

Community Workers
Veterinarians
by Amy McDonald
BLASTOFF! Beginners
BELLWETHER MEDIA
MINNEAPOLIS, MN

Blastoff! Beginners are developed by literacy experts and educators to meet the needs of early readers. These engaging informational texts support young children as they begin reading about their world. Through simple language and high frequency words paired with crisp, colorful photos, Blastoff! Beginners launch young readers into the universe of independent reading.

Sight Words in This Book

a	help	our	to
are	here	some	us
called	how	the	we
do	in	them	
for	is	they	
go	on	time	

This edition first published in 2025 by Bellwether Media, Inc.

Library of Congress Cataloging-in-Publication Data

LC record for Veterinarians available at: https://lccn.loc.gov/2024005405

Editor: Betsy Rathburn Designer: Laura Sowers

Printed in the United States of America, North Mankato, MN.

Table of Contents

Time for
a checkup.
The vet is here!

Respiratory System of the Cat

What Are They?

Veterinarians are animal doctors. They are also called vets.

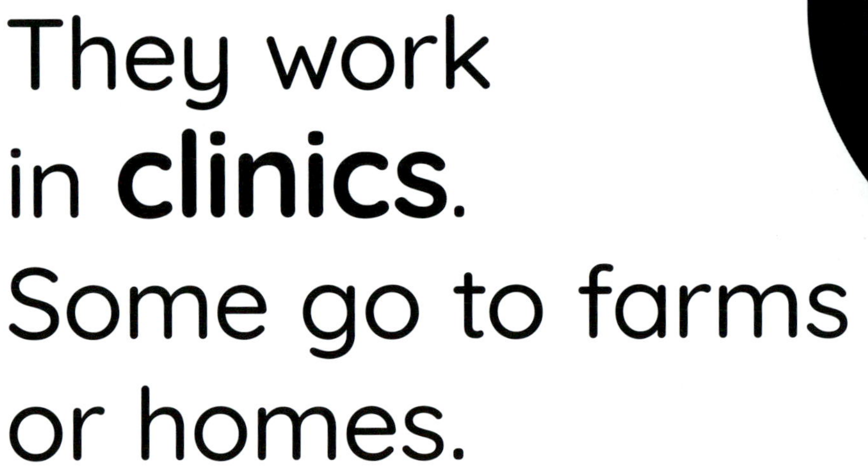

They work in **clinics**. Some go to farms or homes.

clinic

farm

What Do They Do?

Vets keep animals healthy. They do checkups.

They give **shots**.
They clean teeth.

shot

They help
sick pets.
They fix cuts.

They take **x-rays**. They put on **casts**.

taking x-rays

They talk
to owners.
They teach how
to care for pets!

Why Do We Need Them?

We love our pets. Vets help us care for them!

Veterinarian Facts

Tools

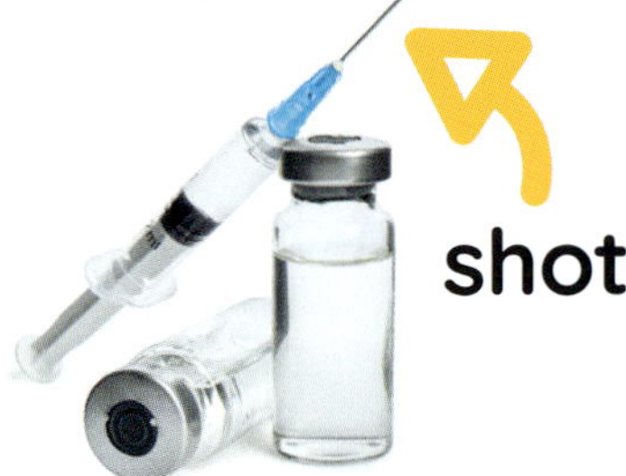

shot

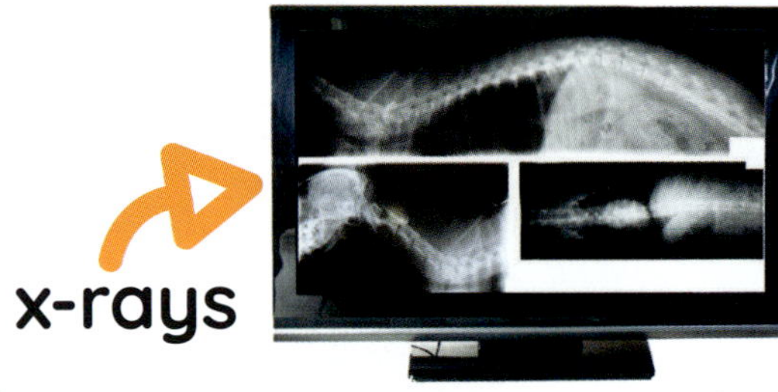

x-rays

cast

A Day in the Life

do checkups

clean teeth

put on casts

Glossary

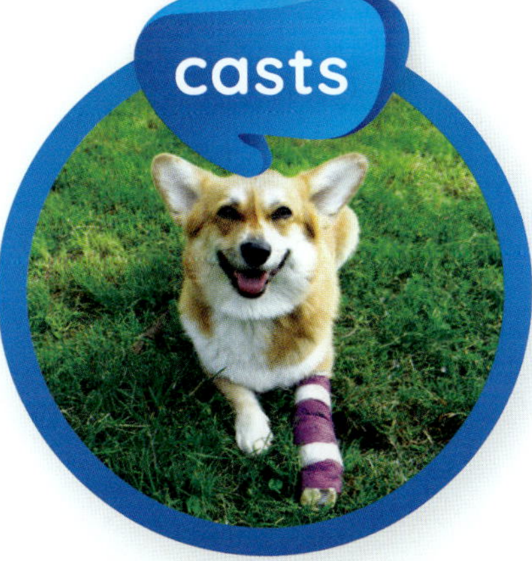

casts

hard coverings used to heal broken bones

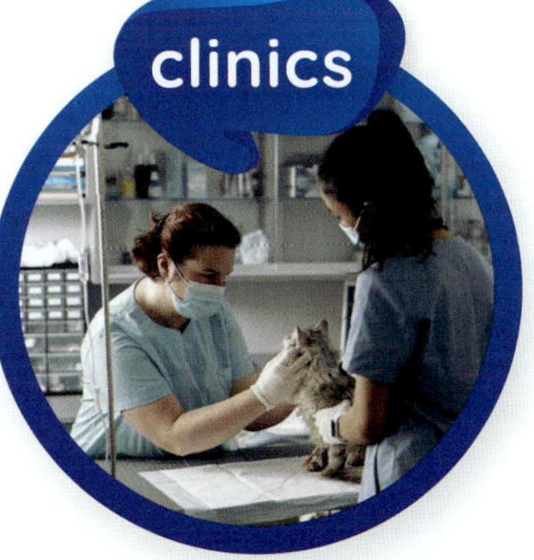

clinics

places that give medical care

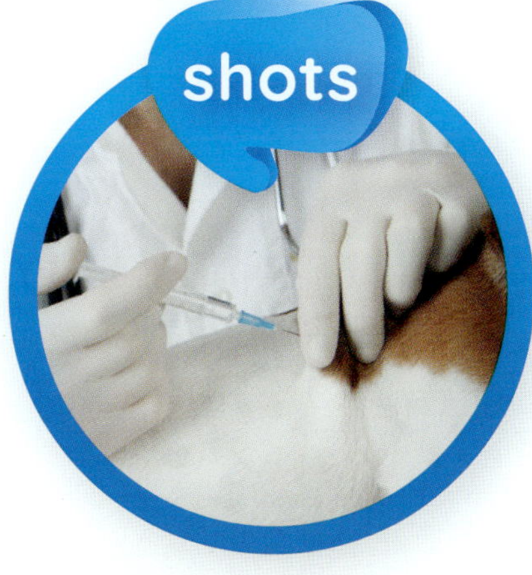

shots

medicines given with needles

x-rays

pictures of inside the body

To Learn More

ON THE WEB

FACTSURFER

Factsurfer.com gives you a safe, fun way to find more information.

1. Go to www.factsurfer.com.
2. Enter "veterinarians" into the search box and click 🔍.
3. Select your book cover to see a list of related content.

Index

The images in this book are reproduced through the courtesy of: Pixel-Shot, front cover; Dragos Vana, p. 3; Rembolle, p. 4; AnnaStills, pp. 4-5; GoodFocused, pp. 6-7; tdub303, p. 8 (clinic); fotopanorama360, pp. 8-9; Maria Sbytova, pp. 10-11; SeventyFour, pp. 12-13; antoniodiaz, pp. 14-15; Eric Isselee, p. 16 (cast); Image Source Trading Ltd, pp. 16-17; Pressmaster, pp. 18-19; Kamira, p. 20; UfaBizPhoto, pp. 20-21; mikeledray, p. 22 (x-rays); New Africa, p. 22 (shots); Paul Vasarhelyi, p. 22 (casts); PeopleImages - Yuri A, p. 22 (do checkups); Andrii Medvednikov, p. 22 (clean teeth); monkeybusinessimages, p. 22 (put on casts); Barbara Strelar, p. 23 (casts); Friends Stock, p. 23 (clinics); Iryna Kalamurza, p. 23 (shots); Ground Picture, p. 23 (x-rays).